I Am Vincent van Gogh

By Gabriel Martín Roig

Illustrated by Fátima García

STAR BRIGHT BOOKS
Cambridge Massachusetts

English text copyright © 2017 Star Bright Books
Illustrations copyright © 2009 Parramón Ediciones, S.A.

Published in English by Star Bright Books in the United States of America in 2017.
Originally published in Spanish as Yo... *Vincent van Gogh* by Parramón Ediciones, S.A.
in Spain in 2009.
Text by Gabriel Martín Roig
Illustrations by Fátima García
Photographs: Agefotostock

The name Star Bright Books and the Star Bright Books logo are registered
trademarks of Star Bright Books, Inc. Please visit: www.starbrightbooks.com.
For bulk orders, please email: orders@starbrightbooks.com, or call customer
service at: (617) 354-1300.

Printed on paper from sustainable forests.

Hardback ISBN-13: 978-1-59572-770-1
Star Bright Books / MA / 00107170
Printed in China / WKT / 9 8 7 6 5 4 3 2 1
LCCN: 2016941548

I Am Vincent
van Gogh

My name is Vincent van Gogh. You may have seen my paintings of sunflowers or starry nights. Thanks to those and my other paintings, today I am probably one of the most famous artists in the world. My life, however, was not easy.

I started painting later than most artists. When I was young, I did not know whether I wanted to be an artist or a minister. In the end, I chose art. With my brush, I created colorful and expressive paintings—ones that were very different from those other artists were doing at the time, making it hard for people to understand my work. I also painted many self-portraits in which you can see me as I was—a very troubled man. Why do I look so unhappy in my self-portraits? If you read my story, you will discover why.

Why was my life so hard? It was mostly because I did not know how to relate to people. I always seemed to do or say the wrong thing, making people angry with me no matter how hard I tried to do the right thing. It was easier just to paint and avoid people even though I was lonely.

While some of my paintings showed how unhappy I was, painting also made me feel better. Focusing on my work made it easier to ignore people when they called me "Crazy Red." This was the offensive name the townspeople of Arles gave me because of my behavior and the color of my hair.

I was never successful during my lifetime. I had my first public recognition at the Salon des Indépendants in Paris in 1890, but I sold very few of my paintings during my life. It was only after my death that my talent was recognized.

Contents

ART, PLACE, AND PEOPLE:
The Making of Vincent van Gogh

A Strict Upbringing

Let me begin my story by telling you about my family and childhood. My father, Theodorus van Gogh, was a pastor of a Protestant church. He was a serious and strict man who was very proud of our ancestry. He often told me about our forbears whom he could trace back to the 16th century.

My mother, Anna Cornelia Carbentus, was a sweet and understanding woman with artistic talent. We lived in a small house in the village of Groot Zundert in the Netherlands, which you may know as Holland.

I was not my parents' first child. Before me, they had another son who died at birth. Exactly one year later, on the same day—March 30, 1853—I was born. I was so weak and thin that my mother doubted I would survive. I proved to be strong, however, and within days my parents gave me the same name, Vincent Willem van Gogh, as their first child who had died. My parents had three girls and two boys after me. My brother Theo, born in 1857, played an important role in my life and work.

My father was stern. He showed little affection for my siblings or me. No one spoke or laughed much in our home. Even as a child, I was often lonely. I played with beetles, spiders, and flowers, spending long hours engaging in imaginary conversations. People in our village wondered about me.

When I was eight years old, my father decided it was time to send me to school. He enrolled me in a school in the village, where I learned French, English, and German. Although I did not enjoy school, far worse was yet to come.

After a while, my father, unhappy with the education I was receiving, decided to employ a governess to teach my sister Anna and me at home. The woman was boring and there were no other children to play with at recess. Each day, I grew unhappier and frequently argued with my father. Two years later, he sent me to a boarding school in Zevenbergen, and after that to the King William II School in Tilburg.

Working at an Art Gallery

At sixteen I had to leave school and go to work because my family was having financial problems. My mother spoke to her brother Vincent whom we called Uncle "Cent." He was an art dealer and a partner at Goupil & Company, an art gallery. With his help, I started working as an assistant in his company in The Hague. I worked there for three years and learned about art, selling paintings, and how to deal with customers.

I did well at my job, and at my request I moved to the London gallery of Goupil & Company, where my uncle was working. It was a much bigger and more important gallery than the one in The Hague. While in London, I visited art museums and signed up for art classes.

After three years in London, my uncle was transferred to the company's gallery in Paris. He asked me if I wanted to join him. I accepted his invitation immediately. Once in Paris, I realized that I was less interested in selling paintings and more interested in creating them. Eventually, I started to get bored at work: I neglected my customers, and argued with them and with my employer. In early 1876, I was let go from Goupil & Company's employment and went home to my parents.

GOUPIL & COMPANY
Art Dealers

With several partners, Adolphe Goupil founded Goupil & Company in the mid-nineteenth century in Paris. Their initial business consisted of publishing and selling reproductions of artwork. When my Uncle Vincent joined as a partner, the company began to buy and sell original paintings, drawings, and sculptures. Later, with an increase in the popularity of photography, they dealt in photographs too. My uncle Cent became a prominent art dealer, and because of him, the company prospered. Over time, Goupil & Company became an important art dealer, with branches in London, Brussels, The Hague, Berlin, Vienna, New York, and Australia.

Portraitist of Misery

When I returned home, I decided to pursue my interest in religion and become a minister like my father. My father encouraged me to join the Faculty of Theology in Amsterdam. In May 1877, I moved to Amsterdam and went to live with another uncle while I prepared for the entrance exam.

I had to study Greek and Latin and that was very difficult for me. Due to my trouble with the two languages and my own lack of effort, I failed my exams. My father was disappointed by my failure and sent me to study in Brussels. There I took a short course in order to become a minister and spread the gospel.

After completing the course in January 1879, I was assigned to my first evangelistic mission in Borinage, a mining village in the poorest region of Belgium. Everyone there lived in the deepest poverty and misery.

I had never seen anything like this before. The miners' degree of poverty made a deep impression upon me. I gave most of my belongings to the needy families there. I shared in their sacrifices, deprivation, and even starvation. During my stay in Borinage, I began to draw the peasants and their lives. I made many drawings of the miners. I was a mostly self-taught artist, learning by observing the people and drawing them. I also copied pages from drawing albums or engravings of famous paintings, like the works of Jean-François Millet. I drew the difficult lives of the peasants, weavers, and miners of the village. I cared deeply about the pain and suffering of the people that I saw around me, and I expressed those feelings in my drawings, completed mainly in shades of black and brown.

I was not satisfied with my work, however, and wanted to learn to draw better. I gave up the idea of being a minister, and in 1880 I enrolled at the Royal Academy of Fine Arts in Belgium. There I learned perspective and anatomy, important subjects for artists. I left the Royal Academy after only a short stay and spent the next ten years drawing and painting.

I Paint for the First Time and Fall In Love

Anton Mauve, a well-known painter who was married to one of my cousins, invited me to move to The Hague. I left the Royal Academy of Fine Arts and went to study with Anton. He told me that we could paint together in his study, but I quietly confessed that...I had never painted!

"Do not worry, I'll show you," he said. Thus, during the winter of 1881 I worked on my first painting, guided by my cousin Anton. Soon I had painted five still life studies and two watercolors. My first paintings were not very good. Done in grays and browns, they were strongly influenced by The School of The Hague, to which Anton belonged. I had much to learn.

My life changed in other ways, too. I fell in love with Clasina Maria Hoornick, who I called Sien. Sien was my model and was featured in my most intense work, *Sorrow*. I loved Sien, but when I told my family about her, they were angry with me. They did not think she was suitable for me. Complaints and reprimands from my parents were constant. The few friends I had stopped talking to me. Finally, I could not endure the situation. I left Sien and The Hague, and went home to my family to reconcile with them and to start over. Again.

Clasina Maria Hoornick often posed for van Gogh

SCHOOL OF
THE HAGUE
Painting Outdoors

Painting outdoors was unusual for an artist when I first started painting. Instead, when learning to draw or paint, students copied drawings, paintings, and sculptures in the studios of the artists to whom they were apprenticed.

My cousin Anton and other artists were interested in the trend toward realism in landscape painting. They chose to do something unusual—they painted outside. Taking their easels and paints along, Anton and the others headed outdoors, where they could paint natural landscapes, just like the French artists of the Barbizon School who minutely observed and painted nature. I too painted outdoors.

The Peasants in Nuenen

I went home for Christmas, a good time of the year to reconcile with family. My parents, who were now living in Nuenen, welcomed me with open arms and convinced me to stay with them. They were worried about me. With their help, I set up a studio in a room off of the presbytery of the Protestant church my father ran. Later, I worked at the home of a Catholic sexton.

My family decided that the best thing they could do for me was to encourage my interest in art. At last I could paint in peace. It felt good to have my family's understanding and support.

During that time, I painted and drew the countryside, houses, churches, and people—farmers and weavers—in Nuenen and its surroundings. In my paintings, portraits of peasants and work scenes abounded. It was in Nuenen that I painted *The Potato Eaters*. This is not a pretty or friendly painting. It shows a peasant family sitting down to a dinner of potatoes and a drink similar to coffee. They are people who have toiled in the field. Their clothes are worn, patched, and dusty. Their skin, dark and rough, has been punished by the sun, wind, and rain. These were not the kinds of paintings other artists were making nor were they paintings people liked to buy to display in their homes.

For two years, things were good until the village priest decided I should not be spending so much time with "people of lower classes," as he put it. The priest even told people not to pose for me. Since this made it impossible for me to find models to paint, I left for Paris.

There is a statue of me in a park in the town of Nuenen.

In the Capital of Art

I was in Paris! I was amazed by the "City of Light." Paris was the art capital of the world and the cradle of Impressionism, a new style of painting. Shortly after arriving, in early March of 1886, I rented a room in Montmartre, a section of Paris where many artists lived. My room was small, but it overlooked a little garden full of ivy and wild vines.

Once settled there, I enrolled in the studio of Fernand Cormon, a leading artist. Every day a model posed for students to sketch. In this way we learned how to draw the human figure. In the afternoons, I made drawings of classical plaster casts of the human body.

During this time, I met other young artists, including Henri de Toulouse-Lautrec and Emile Bernard. I also met Camille Pissarro, Georges Seurat, Paul Signac and above all, Paul Gauguin, with whom I spent the most time.

Paris was the most modern city I had ever seen. Its sidewalks were wide, flanked by rows of trees and surrounded by large blocks of houses and apartments; its streets were full of carriages traveling up and down the avenues; its center was full of art galleries and overcrowded shops. Paris was filled with life and color!

At night, Paris was illuminated with miles of gas lamps, giving it a magical appearance. The city never slept! My brother Theo, his friend Andries Bonger, and I ate at the restaurants of Montmartre almost every night. Sometimes we visited a neighborhood cabaret, Le Chat Noir, to listen to the singing and watch the dancing. I loved living the life of an artist in the amazing city of Paris!

Henri de Toulouse-Lautrec (1864-1901)

The Impressionists!

My Parisian years were the most wonderful of my life. It was there that I met with—and learned from—some of the greatest artists of the time: the Impressionists.

They were painters of light. Instead of using strong lines to make detailed paintings like those of my cousin Anton or the Barbizon School artists, the Impressionists used only pure color to paint images. Color was all that mattered. With loose brushstrokes, they created the impression of shimmering light.

The themes of the Impressionists' paintings also attracted me. They painted subjects such as regattas, picnics, and above all, landscapes. They painted outdoors, just as I liked to do. I, however, did not want to be an Impressionist painter. I adapted certain characteristics of the movement into my own work: their use of vivid and bright colors as well as small, short brushstrokes. It was time to leave behind my dark paintings of the past. Now I wanted to find light through color and movement.

The Impressionist movement showed me the light and the colors around me and helped me define my style.

POINTILLISM:
The Art of Pure Color

One afternoon I went to an exhibition of artwork by Georges Seurat, then a little-known painter. It was a revelation! His style was different from that of the Impressionists. His work did not require the mixing of colors on the palette; instead, he filled the surfaces of his paintings with small dots of color. Thus, if he wanted to create orange, he would fill the area with red and yellow dots. Likewise, if he wanted the color green, he did the same with blue and yellow paint. The viewer's eyes then mixed the various colors, creating the impression of the desired hue in the mind's eye. His paintings were fascinating to look at.

Seurat's style produced a greater degree of luminosity and brilliance of color than I had ever seen before. Gazing at his *Sunday Afternoon on the Island of La Grande Jatte*, I suddenly wanted to use this technique in my own work, but in my own way. I asked the gallery owner if that style of painting had a name. He said it was called Pointillism. Of course, how did I not think of that! Painting with colored dots could only have a name such as that. I thought that I could do something similar. No more stopping to mix colors. Instead, by making small, short brushstrokes of different colors next to each other, I could create the same brilliant effect.

Georges Seurat, Sunday Afternoon on the Island of La Grande Jatte, 1884

My Friend Père Tanguy
and the Japanese Prints

While living in Paris, I bought Japanese prints from a man named Julien Tanguy, who also sold art supplies. Art students and artists affectionately called him "Père Tanguy" because of his age. "Père" is the French word for father. He was more than just a shop owner. The back room of his store became a gathering place for painters. He supported me by exhibiting my paintings in the window of his shop.

More than once, when I had no money, he agreed to take one of my paintings in exchange for canvas and paint. Few people were that kind to me . . . .

To show my gratitude, I made three portraits of Tanguy. I did something very original: I portrayed my friend on a background full of illustrations of Japanese art. Tanguy loved it since he was a dealer of Japanese art.

I loved the Japanese images of the early nineteenth century. I first saw these wood-block prints in Antwerp. The merchant ships brought them over from Asia. Sailors gave them no value and even used them to wrap sandwiches. Only when large exhibitions in London and Paris were held to introduce Europe to these great Japanese artists was their value finally understood. My enthusiasm for this form of art led me to cover the walls of my room with Japanese prints.

In the late nineteenth century, the influence of Japanese art could be seen everywhere. If you took a walk down any Paris boulevard, you would see many decorative items inspired by Japanese and Chinese designs: furniture, painted screens, Chinese vases, and kimono-style clothing. Everyone wanted to buy them!

I was never interested in what was fashionable, but I used these images from Asia to develop my unique style of painting. I carefully chose new points of view, painted large areas of the frame with a flat color, adopted the use of lighter colors, and began to outline the edges of objects with firm strokes or lines. These techniques became defining characteristics of my work.

Facing the Mirror

I was intrigued by the human figure and wished to draw and paint people, but I always had difficulty interacting with others. I rarely had money to pay a model, and it was not easy to find people who wanted to pose for free. For this reason, I had no choice but to get a mirror and become my own model. In addition to always having a face to paint, the self-portrait turned out to be a useful exercise in helping me get to know myself better. I painted many unhappy self-portraits after I left the asylum of Saint-Rémy, where I spent time due to my intermittent health crises. In subsequent self-portraits, I saw the growing signs of my illness, but I could also see my painting skills improving.

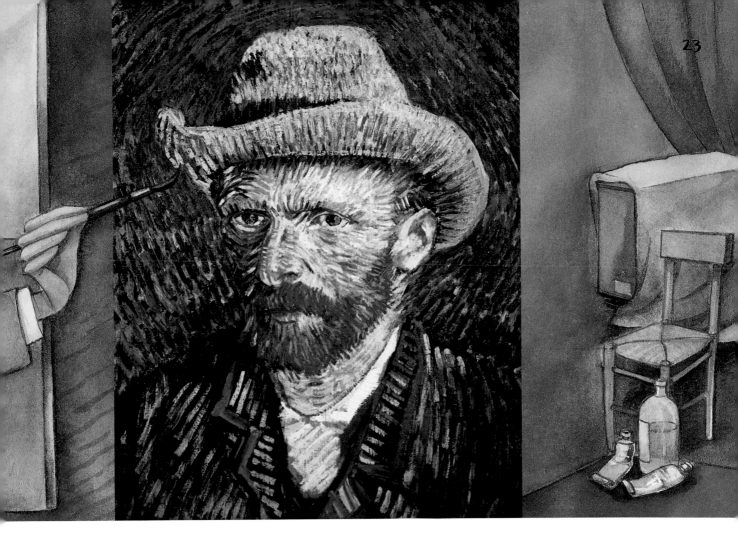

I painted more than thirty-five self-portraits. Some of them I hung in my house in Arles, not because I liked to see my own face, but because I felt lonely. Although it may seem strange, it comforted me to see my own face watching me as I worked. Once I started painting self-portraits, I decided that no one would be allowed to take my photo. People would only know me through my work, through the vision that my own brushes would provide as I looked in the mirror. One day, a friend of Emile Bernard wanted to take my picture. At first I refused, but he insisted. I finally agreed, but on the condition that I would cover my head with a hat and have my back to the camera. That was the last picture that anyone took of me.

Self-Portrait with Grey Felt Hat, 1887

Arles, Sunshine Everywhere

My paintings were now filled with new ideas and intense colors, but I was getting tired of Paris. I wanted to leave the noise and crowds of the city for a more peaceful and sunnier place where I could work outdoors all year round.

Henri de Toulouse-Lautrec, to whom I always told my troubles, suggested that I move to the south of France, where the days are warm and sunlight bathes the countryside. I followed his advice and went to Arles, a small city in the Provence region. Arles was a beautiful place, with a sky of vivid blue, golden wheat fields, and a light so intense it enhanced all of the colors. . . . It was 1888 and I was 34 years old.

The vast fields of Arles reminded me of my native Holland. They fascinated me, and the southern sun renewed me. I felt like a child again, and a great joy came over me.

Never Fitting In

My disconcerting way of acting and my shabby clothes disturbed the people of Arles. I often saw people looking at me strangely or even avoiding me, and I soon found myself isolated. I spent my nights without anyone to talk to, so I passed the time by smoking, drinking, and working. I began painting feverishly. I rose early in the morning, ate breakfast quickly, and carried my easel, canvas, and paints outside to catch the sun and capture the colors of the landscape at their most intense. I found this direct contact with nature soothing.

My long treks to the sunny cornfields and vineyards of Provence were pleasant, and also benefited my health, which had been damaged by years of alcohol abuse and a poor diet. When the sun set below the horizon, I walked back to my rented room with two or three finished canvases. I can never thank my brother Theo for all he did for me during this time. Each month he sent me 250 francs for my meals and expenses, including canvas and paint.

Thatched Cottages and Houses, 1890

A NEW FRAMEWORK
Learning to Draw Using Perspective

During my years in Arles and later in Saint-Rémy, I focused on mastering perspective—the technique of defining space and making shapes look three-dimensional on paper or canvas—and applying it to my work. I had a carpenter build me a rectangular frame that had vertical, horizontal, and diagonal wires within it. Using this, I could determine a vanishing point, the place at which receding parallel lines, seen in perspective, seem to converge. By holding this frame up to the landscape I wanted to paint and looking through it, I could easily sketch the lines, which simplified the drawing process. It was like painting through a window!

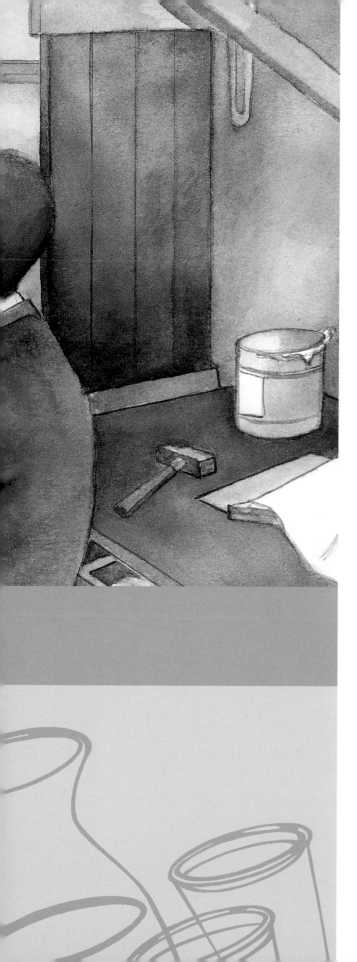

An Explosion of Color

My time in the South of France was a period of light and color. Arles and its countryside, with all of its colorful crops, made me work with brighter paints on my palette. I loved the range of deep, rich blues in the southern sky and the vibrant yellow fields. I do not want you to think that I invented the colors I used in my paintings: these were the colors in front of me. I simply represented them as much more intense. I did not want just to reproduce what I saw. Instead, I used pure and vivid colors to express what I felt about what I was seeing. I used daring, intense colors to communicate the excitement and awe I felt when looking at nature.

When spring arrived in Arles, the fruit trees were covered in blossoms. Their beauty inspired me to find a new way of interpreting light and shadow. I explored the distinct shapes of nature and other objects and how they related to other shapes nearby. I discovered how individual brushstrokes could represent leaves and flowers. Flowering trees soon became one of my favorite subjects.

Sunflowers

Sunflowers are frequently seen in my work. I started painting sunflowers in 1887 while I was still in Paris, first mixed with other flowers and then by themselves. My favorite sunflower paintings, however, are those I completed in Arles between 1888 and 1889 because they remind me of the incredible joy I felt while painting there.

My friend Paul Gauguin planned to visit me in Arles. I wanted him to see the beautiful sunflowers too, so while I waited, I made paintings to show him. Because the flowers wither quickly, I began working each day at sunrise. I only completed four paintings, but they are among my most famous works. In my series of sunflowers, I first presented the flowers as miniature suns spinning on their stems. I then depicted them as fiery masses in motion, their petals like flickering flames. To me, sunflowers had a deep meaning and symbolized life.

I created the sunflowers by using my brush to make small, choppy strokes. For the petals, multiple brush strokes filled with thick paint allowed the flowers to stand out against a flat background color. These strokes give the flowers a strong expressiveness and a sense of movement. I then used a thick line to highlight the profile of each flower. Outlining the flowers was an idea that I got from the Japanese prints I so admired.

Sunflowers, 1888

ARLES
A Place Filled
with Sunlight

Arles was an agricultural town with a rich history. When the Romans settled there, they built many important public buildings, including a theater, a forum, and a magnificent amphitheater much like the Coliseum in Rome. They also built a public bath like the Constantine Baths along the Rhone River.

I admired the splendid portico and cloister of the Cathédrale of Saint-Trophime, which dates from the Medieval Period.

Despite the fact that I did not get along with the people of Arles, posters of my Sunflowers are sold at Arlésien shops, and there is a memorial dedicated to me.

The beautiful Medieval Cathédrale of Saint-Trophime in Arles.

The Yellow House, 1888

The Yellow House

I found a house in Arles that was painted yellow, my favorite color!

For some time, I had looked for a house in Arles with a studio where I could work quietly. I found a home to rent not far from the train station, in a square opposite a small park near the Rhone River. The rooms received a great deal of light, which is perfect for an artist.

I decorated my four rooms with a series of paintings of sunflowers. The sunflowers reminded me of the blazing sun of the Mediterranean coast of France. I wanted the "Yellow House" to be more than my home and my studio; I wanted it always to be the center of a community of artists. Unfortunately, the house was destroyed in 1944 during World War II in an Allied bombing raid.

Yellow became my favorite color and an essential element of the paintings I completed in Arles. Yellow is one of the most difficult colors to use. Second only to white, yellow reflects light to such an extent that it can quickly overwhelm other colors. I chose it because it is the color of the hot sun and the fields of sunflowers that I loved. Besides, since the rooms of my house were painted in shades of blue and violet, yellow paintings contrasted nicely against them.

Left to right :
Cézanne, van Gogh, and Gauguin

POST-IMPRESSIONISM
Towards a New Style of Painting

I am not considered an Impressionist painter, but rather a Post-Impressionist. Post-Impressionism is a term applied to the painting styles of the late nineteenth and early twentieth centuries. It encompasses many personal styles and involves, among other things, a renewed emphasis on the importance of drawing, with a concern for capturing light and the expressiveness of shapes, using brightly colored forms, making thick applications of paint, and using sharp brush strokes. Cézanne, Gauguin, and I are the main figures of Post-Impressionism, which was an important landmark in the history of art. With its innovative approach, it paved the way for avant-garde artistic movements, such as Fauvism, Expressionism, and Cubism.

Bedroom in Arles, 1888

A Famous Bedroom and the Night Sky

One afternoon, I wrote to my brother Theo to tell him that I had made several paintings of my bedroom. I enjoyed painting the room; it was a very interesting thing to do. I stood at one end of the room to paint the scene before me, but I had to change the perspective of the room and the furniture so it would all fit onto the canvas. The walls were pale purple, the floor was painted bricks, and the bed's headboard and chairs were as yellow as fresh butter. The sheets and pillows were a warm lemon yellow while the bedspread was scarlet red. The windows were green. The small table where I washed my hands was orange, and the basin and pitcher, blue. The doors were lilac and next to one door hung a towel.

On the wall there was a rack where I always hung my clothes. To make the space cozier, above my bed I placed some of the portraits I had painted. While the painting looks as if I did not draw the room well, I accurately depicted its uneven corner. This gives the painting a skewed appearance.

I liked my room so much that I painted it from memory even after I left Arles.

The whole time I was in Arles, I was fascinated by the idea of painting night scenes, with the sky full of stars. I wanted to paint the night landscape lit only by the light that it gave off. I had a problem, however: there was little light available from the homes and buildings, and there were only a few gas streetlights in Arles to brighten the night. Painting in the dark, as you can imagine, was difficult to do.

So I invented a strange-looking outfit to solve the problem. I took a sturdy wide-brimmed hat and placed small candles on the front brim. Every evening, I placed my easel on the banks of the Rhone River and lit the candles on my strange hat. The light from the candles gave just enough illumination for me to see my canvas and palette and still make out the colors of the sky. It was somewhat cumbersome to work with that hat on. Occasionally, the hot wax from the candles fell on the palette or, in the worst case, onto my hand, burning me.

Other nights, I walked to the village, where I could sit under the gas lamps to paint the sky that provided such a stunning backdrop to the silhouettes of houses, sidewalk cafes, and nightlife.

As much as I loved the bright, sunny days in Arles, I also loved the glimmering nights. I called this painting *The Starry Night*.

The Starry Night,
1889

Gauguin and I: An Impossible Friendship

On several occasions, I invited Paul Gauguin to visit me at Arles. I even prepared a room for him to stay in at the "Yellow House," which I hoped to turn into "The House of Friends," but he never accepted my invitation. I finally asked my brother Theo to convince Gauguin to visit me.

At last, Gauguin agreed. On October 20, 1888, he arrived. The next two months were pleasant for the two of us: during the day we painted together and at night, we chatted endlessly about art at a nearby tavern.

But our personalities were very different, and we began to argue frequently. Living with Gauguin in our small place began to feel claustrophobic. Our discussions often became arguments.

I remember one time we fought after visiting the Musée Fabre, a museum in Montpellier, France. I told Gauguin how much I liked some of the paintings we had seen there. Gauguin thought the paintings I liked were horrendous, and this prompted a violent argument in the street. People stared at us.

It is hard for most people to understand my relationship with Gauguin. One day we were friends, and the next we were enemies.

PAUL GAUGUIN The Adventurous Painter

Despite how we ended our friendship in Arles, I sincerely think that Paul Gauguin is one of France's greatest painters of the nineteenth century. Gauguin, in my opinion, was a rebel and an adventurer. Throughout his life he traveled to exotic places, first fleeing with his parents from Napoleon III and later visiting, for various reasons, Denmark, Panama, Martinique, Brittany, Tahiti, and the Marquesas Islands. A colorist who used color to great effect, Gauguin was also influenced by Asian art to simplify and flatten his forms. He created wonderful paintings, such as *Vision after the Sermon, Two Women of Tahiti, Where Do We Come From? What Are We? Where Are We Going?*, and *Old Women at Arles*.

Paul Gauguin, *Parau api (Two Women of Tahiti)*, 1892

How I Came to Lose Part of an Ear

I now argued almost daily with Gauguin, ever more violently, until the evening of December 23, 1888, when I lost my temper. Gauguin made me so angry! That's when he told me that he was returning to Paris because he did not want to stay with me another day. I grabbed a razor and threatened him. Gauguin fled the house and stayed overnight in a hotel. I tried to find him, but I couldn't. Back home, my despair caused me to have a panic attack and lose control of myself. To punish myself for driving my friend away, I took a knife and cut off part of my right earlobe.

And What I Did with the Severed Earlobe

I wrapped the piece of my ear, bandaged my head to hide the wound, and presented it to a woman, Rachel, whom Gauguin frequently visited. I asked Rachel to accept the package as a Christmas present. On a note I wrote, "Keep this object carefully." Obviously, I was very ill to have done such a thing to myself and then involve Rachel.

Rachel alerted the police. When they came to my house, I was barely standing because I had lost so much blood. I was near death. I was taken to the hospital, but I hardly remember any of this.

After several days in the hospital, I returned to the "Yellow House" sad and desolate. This was when I started painting empty chairs. They were a symbol of my loneliness.

In the Asylum of Saint-Rémy

After the incident with Gauguin, the people of Arles were upset. They were afraid to have me in their town, and children ran away when they saw me on the street. Some residents demanded that the mayor make me leave the village. When Gauguin returned to Paris, he told my brother that I needed help.

In May 1889, I was admitted to the asylum for the mentally ill in Saint-Rémy in Provence. Again, my brother Theo took care of me: he paid for two rooms, one of which I used for

sleeping and the other — large, sunny, and overlooking the garden — was my studio. It was an isolated place, surrounded by wheat fields, vineyards, and olive groves. My time in Saint-Rémy gave me the opportunity to paint my fellow patients and the gardens and forests surrounding the hospital.

This is the room where I slept in the Saint-Rémy hospital.

The landscape around the hospital was lovely, and gardens surrounding the former cloister encouraged me to work. If I wanted to paint outside, I had to ask for permission. I was allowed to go outside provided that an aide from the hospital accompanied me.

During the year that I spent in the hospital, I painted one hundred and fifty paintings and made hundreds of drawings. I worked tirelessly; however, after experiencing a series of crises and extreme fatigue, I had to stop painting for a while. I could not understand what was happening to me! I could not sleep and experienced hallucinations. The nature of my illness was never fully diagnosed, although some doctors believed that my mental instability was inherited. It was a terrible burden to be so ill in such a way.

At the time, my doctors believed my seizures stemmed from alcoholism, poor nutrition, and schizophrenia, a condition marked by severely impaired thinking, emotions, and behaviors. Not surprisingly, when I entered Saint-Rémy, a doctor lowered my alcohol consumption to a pint daily!

Hospital at Saint–Rémy-de-Provence, 1889

DRAWING WITH REEDS
The Energy of the Short, Thick Stroke

During my stay in Arles and Saint-Rémy, I repeatedly drew the Provençal landscape. As pens, I used sharpened reeds dipped in ink.

The reed pen was more flexible than metal and retained relatively little ink, which was perfectly suited for the short and thick strokes I liked to make. The strokes of the reed pen were very pronounced, making features like clouds, hills, mountains, and vegetation seem sculptural in appearance. The lines looked as if they were fused together, or created with a twisted, textural quality.

Letters to My Brother Theo

Following the brief period when I worked as a preacher, my brother Theo, an art dealer, had financially supported me. He was my closest sibling, and the one with whom I had the best relationship. I had looked after him when we were children, and now, ironically, it was he who took care of me.

Pietà (after Delecroix), 1889

I began to write letters to Theo in August, 1872 when he went to study in Oisterwijk. I did not stop writing to Theo until my death. I sent more than 600 letters to him. Since I did not have many friends or people to talk with, Theo became my best friend and confidant. I told him about my experiences, my disappointments, my failures, my hopes. These letters were a way of reminding myself that someone cared about me. The letters also helped me to collect my thoughts, especially on those days when I was manic or depressed. Together, the letters are an extraordinary documentation of my life, providing insight into how I approached my art and creating a careful catalog of all of my work. I would include cards with sketches or drawings intended to describe each of the paintings that I made. There were few cameras in those days, and the photography process was expensive and slow.

I never mailed my last letter to Theo. I wrote it in the last days of my life, and it was found in my jacket pocket on the day I died. In it I wrote, "In my work, I risk my life and it is the reason I am half-sunk."

I Like to Paint Cypresses

After repeatedly painting the cloister gardens at the asylum in Saint-Rémy, I began to paint the cypress trees that grew around the center. I no longer painted sunflowers; cypress trees now fascinated me. I was interested in achieving an effect similar to my paintings of sunflowers. Thus, for a time, these perpetually green trees became nearly the only subject of my work.

I was enthralled by the shady avenues surrounded by these trees, their branches like black flames quivering in the hot midday sun. In my paintings of cypresses, the trees appear to wave and vibrate as if they were in a strong wind, shaken by a fierce upward movement. With my brushstrokes, I stressed this snakelike movement.

The cypress trees were my new obsession after painting the sunflowers series.

Wheatfield with Cypresses, 1889

I preferred to paint the cypress trees on days in which the wind was blowing hard. The wind did not stop me from working: I tied my hat tightly with a ribbon and fixed the canvas to the easel with a rope. Still, painting was not easy. Sand blew in my face and mixed into the paint, but it was worth it. The wind transformed the cypress trees. They lost their stable forms and twisted, writhed, and looked as if they were tongues of fire. The trees, combined with a sky often filled with wild, spiraling clouds, helped to create an intense sense of tension in the paintings.

Olive Grove, 1889

Back North

When I left the hospital of Saint-Rémy, the first thing I did was to take the train to northern France. I arrived in Paris, where my brother Theo lived. After spending three days at his home, my brother suggested that I move to Auvers-sur-Oise, a nearby village where several painters resided. There, I would be in the care of Dr. Paul-Ferdinand Gachet, a famous homeopath and a friend to many of the Impressionists. When I got to the village, I was delighted by what I saw. The landscape of Auvers encouraged me to start painting again. The houses, thatched huts, and wheat fields captivated me. Here, I painted the simplicity of rural life, but this time I did not focus on the farmers.

Village Street in Auvers, 1890

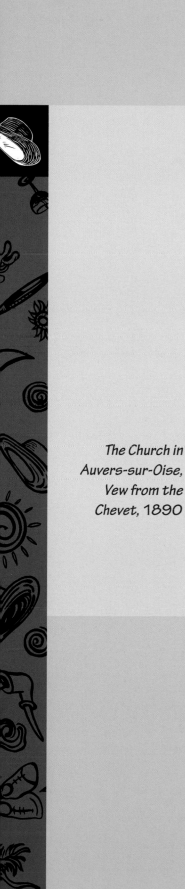

The Church in Auvers-sur-Oise, Vew from the Chevet, 1890

AUVERS-SUR-OISE
Inspired by the River

Auvers-sur-Oise was mainly a farming community with old houses and a peaceful atmosphere, and even now it retains its charm. It attracted many artists over the years, including Charles-Francoise Daubigny, who painted in the Barbizon style, which was a precursor to Impressionism; Camille Pissarro who worked in the Pointillism style; and Henri Rousseau, a naïve painter—an artist who deliberately forgoes the formal rules of painting—who influenced artists such as Marc Chagall, Joan Miro, and Wassily Kandinsky, among others.

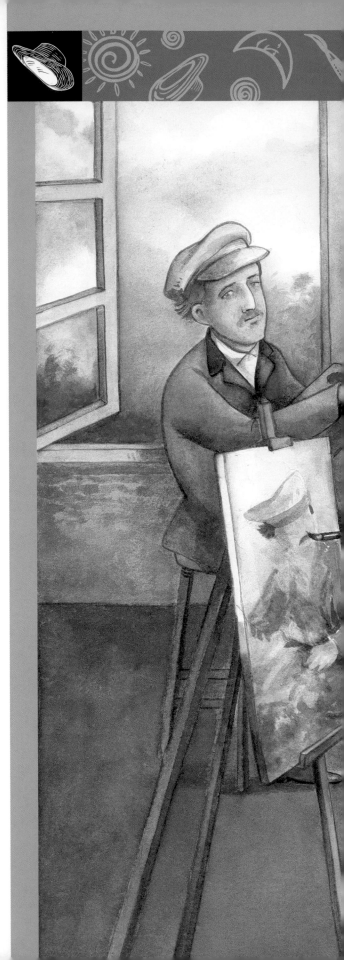

In *Portrait of Madame Ginoux*, I painted the owner of a cafe that I used to frequent in Arles.

At first, everything seemed fine in Auvers-sur-Oise. I worked hard during the day, often making one or two drawings or paintings daily. But in late December of 1889, I suffered another attack while painting. I tried to eat my paints, many of which were poisonous. Luckily, Dr. Gachet was nearby and reacted in time to prevent me from doing so. After that, the doctor forbade me to paint for a few days, so I had to limit myself to drawing on paper. In the months that followed, my anxiety and inner torment guided my hand when painting. I painted and drew as if everything I saw were nightmares—the forms appearing twisted and shaken by a gale. Thus, my strokes spiraled and twisted, and swirls of color began to be characteristic of my pictures.

DOCTOR GACHET
A True Friend

In Auvers-sur-Oise, Dr. Gachet welcomed and looked after me. We had a lot in common, as the doctor was a passionate collector of paintings as well as a painter in his spare time. He encouraged me to continue painting, for he was convinced that the work would be a therapeutic activity. In gratitude, I decided to paint his portrait. The sessions during which the doctor posed for me strengthened our friendship. He was a kind and caring person and admired my painting. In him I found a true friend, something like a new brother.

Wheat Field with Crows

Near Auvers I discovered that during the harvest the great expanses of grain fields attracted large flocks of crows. A month before my death, I painted one of those wheat fields, deserted under a burning sun. Wheat appears to be shaking in the wind while crows fly overhead.

Landscape at Auvers after the Rain, 1890

Van Gogh's grave in a cemetery in Auvers

One day, as the last hours waned, night gained ground, and the sun gave way to the stars, I headed out to paint a wheat field. The wheat was agitated and a dramatic storm was approaching. To paint this picture, I did not use my brushes. Instead, I spread the color with violent and furious movements with a palette knife! Some people claimed that this painting, *Wheatfield with Crows,* predicted my death.

On July 27, 1890, I headed to the wheat fields of Auvers without an easel but with a gun I had borrowed. I said I intended to shoot crows. That afternoon, hallucinations had returned to torment me, and my despair overwhelmed me. It was unbearable.

I gripped the gun. I pointed it at myself and fired the weapon. I wanted a quick death, but it was not to be. Badly wounded, I headed home. Dr. Gachet found me and cleaned my wound, but he could not remove the bullet as it was lodged too deeply. Hearing the news, Theo came to me right away and spent the day by my bed. Two days after the shooting, I died. I was only thirty-seven years old. My brother put my coffin in the room he had rented; my recent paintings covered the walls. He also decorated the room with sunflowers, my favorite flowers.

Sadly, Theo fell ill and died six months later. Since 1914, the two of us have rested together in the cemetery of Auvers-sur-Oise.

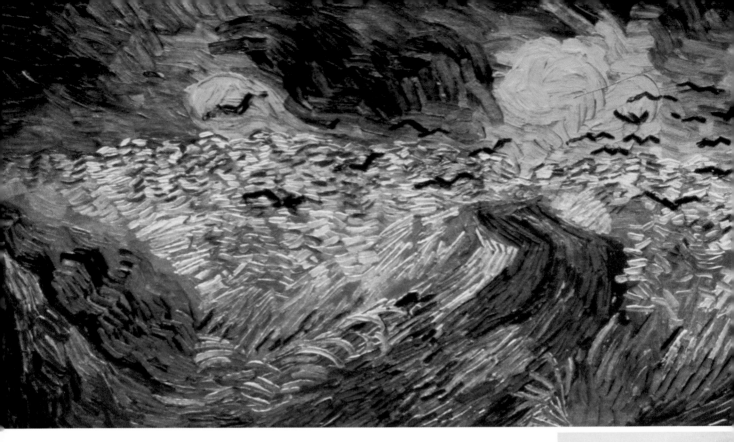

Wheatfield with Crows, 1890

Some believe that *Wheatfield with Crows* predicted how my life would end. They say it perfectly represents the altered mental state I was in days before I shot myself. Some even think it can be seen as a premonition of my death. Perhaps for these reasons, many art scholars consider it "my artistic testament," but for me it was just one more painting. Some writers say that this was my last work, but it is not true. After that painting, I completed a dozen more. I do agree with the assessment that, due to its quality and strength, *Wheatfield with Crows* is one of my best works.

Thatched Cottages at Cordeville, 1890, Musée d'Orsay, Paris

Posthumous Fame

Maybe I was one of the most unfortunate artists of all time. Despite my first public success at the Salon des Indepéndants in Paris, the praise of Camille Pissarro, and the expectations that my paintings aroused in the Hall of Twenty in Brussels in 1890, I did not sell a single painting during my lifetime, except to my brother and Dr. Gachet. It was only after my death that my talent was recognized. The fame I received following my death is thanks to one of the great art dealers of his time, Paul Cassirer. He organized exhibitions of my paintings in Berlin in 1905, at the Museum of Berlin in 1906, at the Great Exhibition of Artists and Friends of Independent Artists from West Germany, and in Cologne in 1912. Cassirer used my work as the main example of the German Expressionist movement. After those exhibitions, my work became a pillar of modern art.

MY MUSEUM
All My Legacy

When I died, my life's work was in the hands of one person, my dear brother Theo. After his death only six months later, my paintings and drawings were passed to his widow, Gesina van Gogh-Bonger. After the death of his parents, my nephew Vincent Willem van Gogh, who was also my godson, inherited and donated the works to the Van Gogh Foundation, founded in 1931 in Amsterdam after an agreement with the city. My artwork and documents were stored first in the Stedelijk Museum for some years. More than 200 paintings, 550 drawings, and 700 letters of mine are now in the Van Gogh Museum in Amsterdam, which opened in 1973. The museum also owns paintings created by my friends and other contemporary artists. The Van Gogh Museum has the largest collection of my art in the world. Over a million and a half people visit the museum every year.

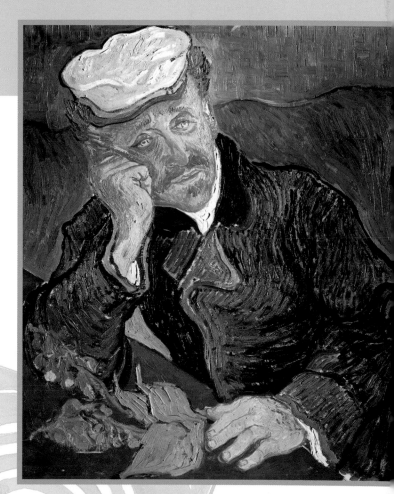

Ironically, today my paintings are sold at prices rivaled by only a handful of other artists, including Pablo Picasso. Between 1985 and 1995, one of my paintings of sunflowers and *Portrait of Doctor Gachet* broke records for the most expensive paintings ever sold up to that time. Paintings that I could not sell in my lifetime are now considered masterpieces.

Portrait of Doctor Gachet, 1890

Life and Times

1853
I was born on May 30 in a village in the Netherlands. That same year the blue jeans manufacturer Levi Strauss & Co. was founded. Giuseppe Verdi premiered one of his most famous operas, *La Traviata*.

1869
I was sixteen years old. I had to leave school and help support my family. I was apprenticed to my uncle at the Goupil Gallery in The Hague. The Suez Canal opened. Monet, Pissarro, and Cézanne began to show their first art works in Paris.

1873
I transferred to the Goupil Gallery in London. Paul Cézanne was a guest of Dr. Gachet, who would become my good friend. Jules Verne published *Around the World in 80 Days.* Claude Monet built a floating studio and painted along the banks of the Seine. In 1874, the first Impressionist painting, *Impression, Sunrise* by Monet, was shown, beginning a new art movement.

1879
I was selected for an evangelizing mission in the Borinage coalfields, where I worked as a preacher for six months. Albert Einstein was born. Edison invented the incandescent lamp.

1880
I took drawing classes in Antwerp, and made numerous sketches of miners inspired by the paintings of Millet. In the fifth Impressionist exhibition, a young Gauguin participated for the first time. Volta invented the first electric battery.

1882
I moved back to The Hague, this time with my cousin, Anton Mauve, also a painter. There, I made my first oil paintings. The following year (1883), forced by poverty, I returned to my family in Nuenen. The Brooklyn Bridge opened, the first exhibitions of Japanese prints opened in Europe, and writer R. L. Stevenson published his adventure story, *Treasure Island.*

1885

In Nuenen, I painted my first major painting, *The Potato Eaters.* After arguments with my family and the village priest, I moved to Antwerp. There, I discovered the work of Rubens and Japanese prints, which impressed me deeply. Pasteur discovered the rabies vaccine.

1886

I moved to Paris, the art capital. There, I enrolled in courses in the painting workshop of Cormon, where I met Toulouse-Lautrec, Pissarro, Seurat, Signac and, most importantly, Gauguin. The last Impressionist exhibition was held in Paris. Sir Arthur Conan Doyle created the character of Sherlock Holmes (1887).

1888

I left Paris and moved to Arles seeking sunlight. There, I created a series of paintings of sunflowers. Soon my friend Gauguin joined me. I suffered a nervous breakdown. The Great Blizzard of 1888 raged in parts of the U.S.

1889

I entered into a mental asylum in Saint-Rémy in Provence, where I spent a year painting garden scenes and cypress trees. In that same year, the Universal Exposition in Paris opened under the metallic structure of the Eiffel Tower.

1890

As my behavior became increasingly unstable, I visited my brother Theo in Paris. He recommended that I go to Auvers-sur-Oise, where Dr. Gachet, with whom I became close friends, could help me. One day in July, I went to paint the countryside and, in a moment of despair, shot myself in the chest. Two days later, I died.

LIST OF PAINTINGS

MUSEUM WEBSITES

You can learn more about the van Gogh paintings you have seen and read about in this book on these museums' websites. Someday, you should visit these museums— there is nothing quite like seeing a masterpiece in person!

Ateneum Art Museum, Finland
www.ateneum.fi/?lang=en

Hermitage Museum, St. Petersburg
www.hermitagemuseum.org/

The Museum of Modern Art, New York City
www.moma.org/

Musée d'Orsay, Paris
www.musee-orsay.fr/en/home.html

The Van Gogh Museum, Amsterdam
www.vangoghmuseum.nl/en

National Museum of Wales, Cardiff
https://museum.wales/